Stephen Curry

The amazing story of Stephen Curry – one of basketball's most incredible players!

Table of Contents

Introduction

Basketball players come and go. We are fortunate to be living in a time when one of the sport's superstars is in his prime for us to witness. Stephen Curry is a boy wonder in the tradition of LeBron James, or his contemporary, Kyrie Irving. As we witness his achievements we can easily dismiss the struggles that he has had to overcome. When we witness a titan in their field, we forget that they came from simple beginnings as we may have had; after all, we only see their triumphs, not the leaps and bounds and hurdles they overcame to reach where they are now. But almost all stories of triumph have modest beginnings, and the story of Stephen Curry is no different.

Only in his thirties, Stephen Curry has achieved in a short span of time what many individuals could not achieve in a lifetime. As the point guard for the Golden State Warriors, he has been recognized as an NBA All-Star, Most Valuable Player, and Champion. His attainments have stretched beyond the National Basketball Association and beyond the United States. He has become one of the world's richest and most recognizable athletes, and he has become a celebrity through both his athletic achievements and his remarkable personality.

This book will take you on a journey, documenting the incredible life and career-to-date of basketball superstar Stephen Curry. Thanks for taking the time to pick up this book – I hope you enjoy it!

Chapter 1: The Early Days

In this chapter, you will learn about Stephen Curry's early life and his beginnings with basketball.

Humble Beginnings

Stephen Curry's journey into basketball stardom seems almost predictable. His father, Dell Curry, was also a professional basketball player for the Cleveland Cavaliers, the Toronto Raptors, and the Charlotte Hornets. At the time of Stephen's birth in 1988, Dell was playing for the Cleveland Cavaliers. Stephen was born in Akron, Ohio, away from the spotlight of Cleveland – and his childhood was not what one would expect from the son of a professional basketball player. Still, like many of his contemporaries, Stephen Curry fell in love with the sport because of his father.

Dell Curry's life began in Grottoes, Virginia. Life in Grottoes was not easy. While Stephen had a proper basket to practice shooting hoops, Dell did not. His father, Jack Curry, created a basket by affixing one to a pole for Dell to practice with. Although this was a substandard basket, it shaped Dell into the talented basketball player he later became.

Dell Curry went on to study at Virginia Polytechnic Institute and State University (Virginia Tech), where he played both basketball and baseball. Though he was adept at both sports, his first love was basketball and he left Virginia Tech as one of its star players. Dell eventually married Sonya Adams. Sonya herself was athletic, playing both volleyball and basketball. With this shared love for athleticism, the pair were made for each other.

In the 1986 NBA Draft, Dell was chosen to play for the Utah Jazz and was traded to the Cleveland Cavaliers the following year. Akron, Ohio became their home, and on March 14, 1988, Dell and Sonya welcomed their first child: Wardell Stephen Curry II.

Though it is unlikely he has any memory of this, Stephen attended one of his father's basketball games at the tender age of two-weeks old. Perhaps subconsciously this left an impression on the young Stephen that would later develop into a love for the game.

Eventually, Dell Curry would leave the Cleveland Cavaliers to join the Charlotte Hornets. The family relocated to Charlotte, North Carolina, where their younger son, Seth, was born. Basketball was the central focus of the Curry family, and young Stephen was enthralled by the sport. However, it took a while for Stephen to master his craft. It may be hard to believe that one of the finest basketball players was once considered a lost cause, but that is the exact situation that Stephen Curry was once in.

While he inherited the love of the sport from both his parents, the physique that Dell Curry possessed did not seem present in young Stephen. He was short and slender. In high school, he stood at 5'6, and was much smaller than any of his teammates. The only comparable basketball player at this height was Muggsy Bogues, who stood at 5'3 and played for the Golden State Warriors. One wonders if during this period, Stephen Curry ever imagined that one day he would play on the same team as Muggsy Bogues. At the time, things may have looked bleak. Although he continued to persevere and was liked by his teammates, his small stature was held against him.

Basketball was not the priority for Sonya Curry, who wanted her sons to have a firm grounding before either of them pursued a professional career. Sonya started a school which her sons attended. Education was the priority for Stephen and Seth; Stephen recalls wanting to watch his father's basketball games at the arena and being prohibited by his mother. On a school night, the priority was to study and get to bed early – attending a basketball game would mean Stephen and Seth would arrive home late. Watching their father play was strictly reserved for the weekends. Education would ensure that Stephen and Seth would be admitted to a great university, and while he may not have realized it then, it would be university where Stephen would get his big break and receive the opportunity to become a professional basketball player.

Church also played a huge part in the Curry household. The school that Sonya established was a Christian Montessori school and Christianity was impressed upon Stephen and Seth at a young age. To this day, Stephen says that he owes much of his success to Jesus Christ.

Moving Up

It was during middle school that Stephen began to shine at basketball. The family had left North Carolina to move even further north. They were living in Toronto, Canada, where Dell Curry played for the Toronto Raptors. Stephen was attending Queensway Christian College, which was not known for its exemplary basketball team. Still, the Queensway Saints are remembered as being the training ground of a young Stephen Curry, and although he managed to cultivate a reputation of success, his time on the basketball team was to be short-lived.

After a successful stint with the Toronto Raptors, Dell Curry retired from basketball, and the family left Canada to settle in the United States for good. They returned to the state where Dell had his most successful time as a basketball player: North Carolina. Stephen began attending Charlotte Christian School and was now more determined than ever to work toward a career as a professional athlete. Stephen had improved tremendously as a basketball player, but there was still much lacking. He was not the best shooter, and this skill needed significant improvement if he was to have any chance of becoming a professional basketball player. He would shoot hoops over a thousand times per day, fighting exhaustion to master his free throws. His frustrations would grow as he missed basket after basket, only occasionally finding success, but gradually he improved. Little did he know that he would eventually become one of the best shooters in basketball history.

Playing on the basketball team for Charlotte Christian School was Stephen's time to shine. He was named Most Valuable Player and helped lead the team to three conference championship wins. Charlotte Christian School's basketball team was called the Knights, and like a knight, Stephen Curry was fierce in his approach to the game. Things were looking up for Stephen, and it seemed that he was on his way to becoming a professional basketball player.

Chapter Summary

• Stephen Curry found his love for basketball through his father.

• He was often met with skeptics due to his small stature.

• He always managed to excel in the sport, despite his limitations.

In the next chapter, you will learn about Stephen's time in college and how this helped him on his road to professional athletics.

Chapter 2: Better Things To Come

In this chapter, you will learn about how Stephen excelled with the Davidson Wildcats and how this would lead to him joining the NBA.

The Wildcats

Although Stephen was a star player for the Knights, he did not receive a basketball scholarship from any major university. Stephen was crushed, as was his family. In spite of his achievements, basketball recruiters were hesitant to give him an opportunity to play the sport for their schools. While he was now six feet tall, this was still significantly shorter than the almost giant-like physiques of his contemporaries. He was also much skinnier.

His dream had been to follow in his father's footsteps by attending Virginia Tech University, but he was not offered a scholarship by the institution, and that dream was crushed. Instead, he was to stay in North Carolina, and he went on to attend Davidson College, a small private liberal arts college. The school did not have a prestigious basketball program. Of course, neither did Queensway Christian College, but this did not prevent Stephen from excelling and improving his craft.

A pattern was present in Stephen Curry's career so far. He was a kind of underdog, with a stature not on par with his teammates. The teams he played on were also underdogs, and it was under his leadership that the teams were brought into the spotlight. Davidson College's team had not won a basketball championship since 1969. However, the Wildcats' coach, Bob McKillop, had tremendous faith in the young Stephen. He saw a warrior-like quality in Stephen and felt that Stephen could excel in the sport in spite of his small stature. Part of the discipline which Stephen still has is due to the toughness of Bob McKillop. Bob ensured that Stephen would not show up late to practice and would play basketball well-beyond the allotted training hours. When Stephen was ready for his first collegiate basketball game, Bob was eager to announce to the world that they were going to witness something special.

Stephen, now christened "Steph," thanks to Bob McKillop, was finally in the spotlight, though there was still much that needed improvement. The Wildcats' first game against the Michigan Wolverines resulted in a loss. Steph was a weak point guard; he had difficulty controlling the ball, and his opponents dominated him. There was much work to be done, but Steph was determined to lead Davidson to success.

Next, the Wildcats played against Central Connecticut State and defeated them 91-64. Steph Curry was responsible for much of this. It seemed the endless shooting practice had finally paid off. Slowly but surely, Davidson was on the road to a championship. The Wildcats had significantly improved as a team and Steph Curry was one of their star players. On February 6, 2007, Steph broke the scoring record for a freshman at Davidson – he had scored a total of 502 points since his college career began. The skeptics who had balked at his short stature were eating their words; it was apparent that Steph Curry was a force to be reckoned with. The Davidson Wildcats joined the NCAA tournament and had set a place for themselves amongst the top collegiate basketball teams.

Steph Curry went on to become the star of the Davidson Wildcats and one of the top collegiate-level basketball players. By his senior year, he decided not to continue at Davidson, as he had bigger plans. Steph had overcome the odds and was now considered a suitable choice for the National Basketball Association.

Chapter Summary

• Stephen did not find acceptance in any of his desired colleges; he settled with Davidson instead.

• He helped bring the Wildcats into the spotlight.

• He became the star of the team, and his accomplishments did not go unnoticed.

In the next chapter, you will learn about Stephen's early career in the NBA.

Chapter 3: The Professional

In this chapter, you will learn about Steph's early days with the NBA and a rivalry which would make history.

NBA Draft

It was a typical New York summer. The city teemed with the usual hustle and bustle and the air was charged with excitement. The WaMu Theatre at Madison Square Garden was packed with part-excited, part-anxious collegiate-level basketball players and their families. It was the National Basketball Association's 2009 Draft, where top-level collegiate basketball players were to be chosen to play for professional NBA teams. Among the young men was twenty-one-year-old Steph Curry of the Davidson Wildcats. Steph Curry had an impressive resume – in spite of his short stature in comparison to other players (he was now 6'3), he had managed to overcome the odds and lead the Davidson Wildcats to many victories. Without a doubt, he was the best player the Wildcats had ever had. As he sat with his family, he eagerly and nervously anticipated what was to come.

His father, as you will recall, had played for several basketball teams – most notably, the Charlotte Hornets. One of his teammates during his stint with the Hornets was the diminutive but fierce Muggsy Bogues. The young Steph saw a role model in Muggsy. Despite standing only 5'3, Muggsy made a name for himself in basketball. While Steph had grown to over six feet tall, he was still considered shorter than most basketball players. He was determined to make an impact on professional basketball in the same manner that Muggsy did. Little did Steph Curry know that though he was from North Carolina, he would become the pride of Oakland, California.

The 2009 NBA Draft got underway and six players were chosen for their respective teams: Blake Griffin for the Los Angeles Clippers; Hasheem Thabeet for the Memphis Grizzlies; James Harden for the Oklahoma City Thunder; Tyreke Evans for the

Sacramento Kings; and Ricky Rubio and Jonny Flynn for the Minnesota Timberwolves.

One can only imagine the state that Steph Curry was in. With each name call, he must have wondered when – even if – he would hear his own name. His father must have been just as anxious as he eagerly awaited to hear his son's fate.

Although what was going through Steph's mind is a mystery, one can surmise that his mind was racing with memories of his basketball career so far: begging his mother to attend his father's basketball games, shooting hoops relentlessly, leading his middle and high school teams to glory, leaving college as the finest player the Davidson Wildcats ever had. What was to become of him now? Wildcats coach Bob McKillop insisted that Steph Curry was something special. Would anyone else think the same?

Steph Curry was the seventh pick of the 2009 NBA Draft and was selected as point guard for the Golden State Warriors. Tumultuous applause erupted and echoed throughout the WaMu Theatre when his name was called. He was now a professional basketball player, and as he looked back on his career so far, he felt there were only things to look forward to.

However, his selection by the Golden State Warriors was met with skepticism. The Warriors had already chosen one smaller player: Monta Ellis. Though Monta was a skilled player, there was much speculation on how two smaller players would benefit the Golden State Warriors; how could both Monta Ellis and Steph Curry stand up to the larger players on the opposing teams? Steph himself was unsure at first if he wanted to play for Golden State, as he would not be in the spotlight as much. But the decision was made, and he was determined to see his team win. After all, it had become a pattern in Steph Curry's career: he had been chosen for less-prestigious teams but managed to lead them to victory.

A Golden State Warrior

On October 28, 2009, just four months after being recruited into the National Basketball Association, Steph Curry played his first professional game with the Golden State Warriors against the Houston Rockets. Though this game ended in a one-point loss, 108-107, and Steph expressed his disappointment and nervousness, his adeptness did not go unnoticed. He managed to score 14 points and helped his team keep up with the Rockets until the very end. Fans were eager to see what Steph Curry would show them.

In spite of the excitement surrounding Steph's initial performance, he had yet to win the team or the fans over completely; just as his celebrity and prowess in his high school and collegiate teams came gradually, so would the opportunity to make a name for himself in the professional sphere. His independence and ability to lead weren't really recognized until the New Year, when Monta Ellis injured himself and sat out two games. It was during these two games that Steph Curry got to show his true capabilities.

The Golden State Warriors defeated the New Jersey Nets in January 2010, 111-79. In the next month, they managed to massacre the Los Angeles Clippers, 132-102. Much of their success in these two games was due to Steph. He was gaining a reputation with his teammates and with basketball fans alike, but he knew that he still had a long way to go, and had to make his presence known as much as possible.

One of the biggest challenges that Steph faced as an up-and-coming basketball star was his shooting. However, his shooting had increased tremendously since joining the Golden State Warriors. With each game, win or lose, Steph was able to practice his shooting – from the field, his accuracy was 46% and from the three-point range his accuracy was 43%. As a result, Steph was selected to participate in the 2009 NBA All-Star Weekend. He competed in the Three-Point Shootout competition and excelled, coming in second by only three points to the Boston Celtics' Paul Pierce.

And the accolades kept coming. In 2011, Steph was honored with being part of the NBA All-Rookie First Team and was awarded the NBA Sportsmanship Award. He was nearing his twenty-third birthday and was no longer a rookie in the world of professional basketball. It seemed as if this underdog was gradually rising to the top. However, Steph could not have anticipated the obstacle that would soon impede his rise to stardom.

The intensity with which Steph Curry played caught up to him. He felt pain in his right ankle during several games. The pain was excruciating, but the injury was even worse than he had imagined: his right ankle was riddled with torn ligaments and he needed surgery to repair them. While he wished to ignore the doctor's orders and continue to play, he was unable to perform with the injured ankle. Much to his chagrin, he had to step aside and miss several games.

Sitting out for a few games may not seem like a huge issue, but it certainly was for Steph Curry. After all, basketball players come and go – and many of them come and go in a flash. Steph had barely won over his teammates and the Golden State Warriors' fans. As he sat on the bench due to his injury, other stars began to shine. Many of his contemporaries were occupying the spotlight Steph had hoped was meant for him. The formidable James Harden was a dominant force in the game – first with the Oklahoma City Thunder and later with the Houston Rockets. One of Steph's longtime adversaries was Kevin Durant – who held the record for freshman scoring as a collegiate-level basketball player. Kevin Durant was also on the Oklahoma City Thunder and went on to be named the Most Valuable Player at the 2012 NBA All-Star Game. He also became the youngest player in the history of the sport to join the 50-40-90 club, reserved for those receiving 50% in field goals, 40% in three-pointers, and 90% in free throws.

With these two kings reigning over the court, Steph Curry's achievements seemed to dwindle. Although he must have felt defeated as he sat helplessly on the bench, he would reclaim the spotlight thanks to another player. After Steph Curry was picked in the 2009 NBA Draft, the eighth, ninth, and tenth players were chosen for their respective teams. The eleventh pick was to join the Golden State Warriors, as well. His father, Mychal, had been an accomplished basketball player, and he was determined to follow in his father's footsteps. Klay Thompson was another player whose talents were met with skepticism, but working alongside Steph Curry, the two would become living legends.

2011

On Christmas 2011, Steph Curry was back in the game; however, it seemed that he had not fully recovered. The Warriors faced a humiliating loss to the Clippers with an 86-105 final score. Over the course of the game, Steph managed to score a measly four points. It was hard to believe that this was the same Steph Curry who wowed fans in his first game with the Warriors. The injury had done its damage. Fans and critics wondered whether Steph Curry would ever make a comeback.

2011, however, was not completely a dark time for Steph Curry. Apart from basketball, he now had a new love in his life.

As a commitment to Christianity was an important facet of Steph's upbringing, he and his brother Seth were active in their local church's youth group. As a teenager, Steph met a young girl at his youth group whom he was immediately smitten by. The girl, Ayesha Alexander, and Steph hit it off immediately. However, their friendship was short-lived as Ayesha soon moved to Los Angeles where she would act in a variety of television shows.

After completing high school, Steph took a chance and searched for his long-lost love on Facebook. His leap of faith was rewarded. He found Ayesha and the two reconnected after many years. In 2011, Steph and Ayesha were married, and later had two daughters, Riley and Ryan. Steph is a dedicated family man, and in spite of the fame he has achieved, he ensures that his family remains the central focus of his life.

In 2011, he also completed some unfinished business. He had forgone his senior year at Davidson to enlist in the NBA Draft. While his family was pleased, as was he, there was something missing. Steph remembered that as a child his mother forbade him and his brother from attending their father's basketball games during the week, as getting rest for school the next day was the priority. As basketball had taken precedent during his adulthood, Steph had left Davidson without completing his degree. During his time off court, whilst recovering from his injury, Steph decided to return to Davidson to complete the remaining coursework. He managed to complete the necessary coursework and received his Bachelor of Arts degree in Sociology. During his return to Davidson, he reunited with Bob McKillop, his collegiate basketball coach who had had tremendous faith in him and had known that the young Steph would become a star.

In spite of his injury, Steph worked alongside Bob McKillop and helped coach the current roster of the Davidson Wildcats. The players must have been ecstatic that a professional basketball player was teaching them a thing or two about the sport. Just as Dell Curry and his teammates had a profound influence on Steph and his brother Seth as they were growing up, Steph was able to reciprocate this with the Davidson Wildcats.

The poor performances on the court due to his injury would continue into the New Year as the Golden State Warriors lost to both the San Antonio Spurs and the Indiana Pacers. However, the relentlessness that Steph Curry possessed was soon to make an appearance again. Against the Portland Trailblazers toward the end of January, Steph was vicious. He managed to score 32 points and even steal the ball four times. The game was close, but due to Steph's skill, the Golden State Warriors defeated the Portland Trailblazers 101-93. The feat was repeated with a game against the Utah Jazz, defeating them 119-101. Although a later game against the Memphis Grizzlies was lost by a mere point, Steph's impeccable leadership managed to show the fans that he was back in the game.

2012

Four days before his twenty-fourth birthday, things took a turn for the worse. His foot was sprained once again, and he had to undergo a second surgery. In spite of this new setback, the faith in Steph Curry had not faded. One individual who particularly believed in Steph was the Golden State Warriors' general manager, Bob Myers. Bob Myers wanted Steph Curry to be the central focus of the Golden State Warriors. He knew that regardless of what obstacles came his way, Steph Curry was destined for greatness.

Monta Ellis was no longer a player for the Golden State Warriors – he had been traded to the Milwaukee Bucks. Mark Jackson was the current Warriors coach, and in spite of having a troubled season, he was determined to lead them to the NBA Championship. Steph's ankle was healing after receiving surgery. While part of him was nervous and unsure of whether or not he would succeed, his relentlessness pushed him to continue; he was determined to bring the Golden State Warriors to the NBA Championship.

2012 was not the best year for the Warriors or for Steph. But he was intent on making 2013 the year that he and his team would rise to greatness. He befriended one of his newest teammates, the inimitable Klay Thompson. Steph was initially hesitant to join the Warriors, but his viewpoint had now changed. In the Oakland-based team, he found a family. Sure, the Warriors were underdogs in the NBA, but Steph had spent his entire basketball career helping underdog teams rise to the top. He was going to make his family proud.

Chapter Summary

• Though it was not his first choice, Stephen came to love the Golden State Warriors

• Stephen's early career with the Golden State Warriors was promising

• Stephen's injuries did hinder his progress and his rise to the top

In the next chapter, you will learn about the road to the 2017 NBA Championship.

Chapter 4: Becoming A Champion

In this chapter, you will learn how Stephen led the Golden State Warriors to the NBA Championship.

2015

Steph Curry was now a seasoned basketball player. He was the pride of the Golden State Warriors and this young man from North Carolina had become one of Oakland, California's most popular residents. In his professional career so far, Steph had experienced ups and downs. The year 2015, however, would be one of the highlights of Steph's career and unbeknownst to him, would begin a short-yet-significant era in the history of the game.

The 1975-1976 season had been the best season for the Golden State Warriors thus far. While they did not win the NBA Championship, they won a total of 59 games. This season seemed to be the zenith that the Golden State Warriors had reached. It was the peak of their success, and many critics would say that 1975-1976 was the season that could not be surpassed.

Mark Jackson was no longer the coach of the Golden State Warriors. He had been replaced by Steve Kerr, who was new to serving as a head coach of a team. However, Steve had an impressive history. He had been a successful basketball player and had won five NBA Championships with the Chicago Bulls and the Phoenix Suns. As a coach, he was determined to lead the Golden State Warriors to their first NBA Championship.

Steve Kerr emphasized improving the Golden State Warriors' offense. If they wanted to win an NBA Championship, they had to be as strong on their offense as they were on their defense. Scoring points and making baskets was as crucial to their success as was defending against their opponents. Steph Curry had to significantly improve his shooting. This had been the challenge of his career – both as an amateur and as a professional. He would have to help his teammates score as many points as possible to make it to the playoffs and eventually win the NBA Championship. Steph took this challenge to heart and went on to score 286 three-pointers, setting an NBA record.

Steve Kerr's leadership proved invaluable. The Golden State Warriors had now gained a notoriety which they had not held for years. It seemed that they were going to break the supposed plateau they had reached in the 1975-1976 season.

On June 4, 2015, the Golden State Warriors were ready to play their first game of the 2015 NBA Finals. Their adversary was the Cleveland Cavaliers. Oddly enough, the Cleveland Cavaliers had a place in Steph Curry's heart. This was one of the teams that his father Dell had played for decades prior. The Cavaliers were a stellar team and were led by the masterly LeBron James. The team's point guard, Kyrie Irving, was also turning heads and, as Steph's contemporary, was his immediate adversary. Heated debates were exchanged as to who was the best point guard. Steph had accumulated a legion of supporters who would argue that it was him; however, so had Kyrie Irving. Steph was determined to not only help the Golden State Warriors win the NBA Championship, but to also solidify his place as the NBA's foremost point guard. The Cleveland Cavaliers may have been a team he admired as a child, but it was now his mission to defeat them.

At the start of the first game, things were looking pretty bleak for the Warriors. The Cavaliers remained ahead at the end of the first quarter. The Warriors realized that they had to go on the offensive. The Warriors came back with a vengeance. In the second quarter, they managed to increase their score, but the Cavaliers were ahead with 51 points to the Warriors' 48. The Cavaliers were also on the offensive and the two teams were playing aggressively; they both had one agenda – to win the NBA Championship.

It was the fourth quarter. Both teams were playing combatively. As Steph attempted to score, he was blocked by none other than Kyrie Irving. The scores were tied, and the game went into overtime. The Warriors had run out of patience. They scored 10 points that put them miles ahead of the Cavaliers. Their defense was also strong – though the Cavaliers did score during the overtime quarter, they were no match for the fierceness of the Warriors. The Warriors had won the first game of the 2015 NBA Finals.

Game 2 seemed to be a repetition of the first game. The score was once again tied in the fourth quarter. This time, however, the victory went to the Cavaliers. Despite the absence of Kyrie Irving, Steph Curry did not manage to be the top scorer for this game. LeBron James seemed to have taken the initial defeat personally as he managed to dominate the Warriors and lead the Cavaliers to victory. The wins were now tied, and it was anyone's guess which team would win the 2015 NBA Championship.

The third game must have annoyed Steph greatly. Though he managed to score 27 points for the Warriors – the top scorer for his team – it was insufficient. The game was a close one, but the Cavaliers managed to defeat the Warriors 96-91. The glee that the Warriors and Steph felt from winning the first game had rapidly faded away. The Cavaliers were in the lead and the intensity of LeBron James had overpowered the adeptness of the Warriors. Steph needed to up his game if he wanted the Warriors to win the Championship.

To state that Steph improved his game on June 11, 2015 would be an understatement. He and teammate Andre Iguodala managed to score 22 points each. In every single quarter, the Warriors were in the lead. Though the Cavaliers put up a good fight, it was clear that the game was in the Warriors' favor. The Warriors ended the game with 103 points, leading by a large margin to the Cavaliers' 82. The two teams were tied in the series, and the stakes could not have been higher.

Game 5 was a tense match. Both teams needed to win this game to secure the lead. Each time a team scored, it seemed that the other team matched it. However, Steph remembered his coach's desire for the Warriors to improve their offense. Steph, who once struggled with shooting, was now an expert shooter. He managed to score 37 points in the game, and in the fourth quarter, he was a driving force in bringing the Warriors to the lead. It was a close game, but the Warriors claimed victory. Though they were overjoyed, Steph knew that it was still perhaps premature to celebrate. If the Cavaliers won Game 6, the scores would be tied, and a seventh game would be called for. Steph was determined to end the finals with Game 6 and win the Championship.

While the Warriors were in the lead for the first two quarters of the sixth game, the Cavaliers had put up a great fight in the second quarter. There was no room for the Warriors to get comfortable. The Cavaliers had a strong defense as well as a strong offense. The entire Warrior team would have to stand up to the force that was LeBron James. Repeating the pattern from the fourth game, Steph and Andre scored the highest points for the Warriors, with 25 points each. Steph realized that though LeBron was an intimidating force, cooperation with his teammates could help them overtake LeBron. Teamwork and collaboration paid off. The Cavaliers played well, but the Warriors played just a bit better. The sixth game was over. The 2015 NBA Finals were over. The Golden State Warriors had defeated the Cavaliers in game six, 105-97.

Steph Curry had led the Golden State Warriors to win the 2015 NBA Championship against the Cleveland Cavaliers. This was an incredible feat and would be the start of a long rivalry between the two teams. Steph Curry had much to celebrate; as a diminutive amateur basketball player, he helped his underdog school and collegiate teams rise to greatness. He could have never imagined he would take the Golden State Warriors this far – all the way to an NBA Championship. However, the celebration would not last forever. The loss to Golden State was harrowing for the Cleveland Cavaliers and they were intent on playing in the finals again – this time to win.

2016

Steph had signed a contract with the Warriors to keep him part of the team until the 2016-2017 season. Choosing to play for another four years with the Warriors showed his commitment to the team. Barely into the New Year, the Golden State Warriors played the Los Angeles Clippers. Steph managed to score 31 points in the game – an incredible feat for someone who had spent more time off court than on in the past year. He had eight attempts at the three-point-range and managed to score on six of them. Shooting had been Steph's greatest challenge as a novice, but it seemed things were improving.

He once again led the Warriors to victory as they defeated the Portland Trail Blazers on January 11. Fans were overjoyed to see their new hero Steph Curry back in action. Steph, too, was feeling enthralled by the support. He had been granted the same allure that legendary Basketball players from Michael Jordan to Muggsy Bogues had been given – his fans wanted him to lead the Golden State Warriors to an NBA Championship. He was the central focus of the team, and he had a lot of responsibility on his shoulders.

2016 was an exciting year for the Golden State Warriors and for Steph Curry, but ultimately it ended in a disappointment. The Golden State Warriors had made it to the 2016 NBA Playoffs. This was what Steph had hoped for. He was known to have a Midas Touch; it was his leadership which would bring underdog teams to glory. Such was his intention in 2016. The Golden State Warriors were up against the Cleveland Cavaliers. The Cavaliers had perhaps the most formidable player in the NBA, LeBron James, leading them. They also had one of Steph's contemporaries – another stellar point guard, Kyrie Irving. The teams went head-to-head, and although Golden State had managed to lead in the first two games, Cleveland caught up in Game 3. Golden State bounced back and won Game 4. Cleveland then won Games 5 and 6. Then, the final game arrived. Steph Curry had been one of the highest scorers of each game and was determined to win the Championship.

The pressure could not have been more immense. Whichever team won Game 7 would become the 2016 NBA Champions. The game was close, but it was not one where Steph Curry shined. He had managed to lead as the top scorer for three of the games, but this one was led by Draymond Green, who even managed to surpass top scorer LeBron James. However, his efforts would prove to be futile. Within the last few minutes of the game, Golden State was down by four points. The game could not have been closer. With the time expiring, the ball was with Steph Curry. He planned to shoot a three-pointer; this would bring Golden State closer to Cleveland, and if they were lucky, they could score one more basket. He had improved tremendously as a shooter, even winning the NBA's three-point competition. This time, however, it seemed fate was not on Steph's side. The bad luck with three-pointers he had as a novice player came back to haunt him. He aimed the ball, shot, and watched in trepidation and then agony as the ball steered clear of the basket.

The time was up. The 2016 NBA Champions were the Cleveland Cavaliers and the celebrations were immense. LeBron James, the hero of the NBA, had led his team to victory. Eyes were also on the young Kyrie Irving. To top it off, Game 7 received the 2016 ESPY Award for being considered the best game of the year. It certainly was a spectacle and one of the most entertaining games basketball fans had seen in a long while. There was a prevalence of excitement in Ohio, but in Oakland, California fans and players alike hung their heads in shame. No greater shame however, was present than in the point guard who felt he had failed his team. Steph Curry had failed in securing the NBA Championship for the Golden State Warriors. He was to return home, empty-handed.

One can only guess what thoughts were rushing through Steph Curry's mind during the night he returned from the 2016 NBA Championship's final game. He had recovered from an injury a few years prior, and although his ankle gave him trouble on and off, he had managed to win several games with the Golden State Warriors. He had become the central focus of his team and fans and pundits had now claimed him as one of the most exciting players in the NBA.

Though many of his thoughts may have been negative, Steph had worked too hard to let his team and his fans down. Somewhere in his mind, he must have remembered watching his father play as a child. Steph had marveled at Dell's skill and hoped to become a great basketball player just like him. As a young player, Steph had all the odds stacked against him. He was short and skinny. He had no particular skill with the sport, he was no match for the larger and bulkier opponents, and at the time he couldn't shoot particularly well. Yet, Dell Curry never gave up on his son. He was determined to mold Steph into a great basketball player. At times, Steph would tire of practice; but nonetheless, he was relentless and would shoot hoops until his arms were aching.

He also found comfort in Jesus Christ. He was raised to believe that he would find success if he kept his faith strong and he never wavered in that faith. With the support of Christ, his family, his teammates, and his fans, Steph Curry was determined to redeem himself. He had one goal in mind: He was going to lead the Golden State Warriors to another NBA Championship win.

2017

It was 2017. The Golden State Warriors had come back from an incredible season which unfortunately ended in a Game 7 loss by a mere four points in the NBA Championship. The Warriors watched with disappointment as the Cavaliers and their fans celebrated their victory. The Warriors were not willing to let this slide; after all, a true Warrior is always ready for another battle. The team was now under the dual coaching prowess of Steve Kerr and Mike Brown, who were eager to regain the spotlight from the Cleveland Cavaliers. They had also added superstar Kevin Durant to their team during the offseason, and were now more formidable than ever!

This year marked the third consecutive year that the Golden State Warriors were to compete in the NBA Playoffs. They were determined to play in the NBA Finals and redeem themselves after their painful and embarrassing loss to the Cleveland Cavaliers the year before. Perhaps none of the Warriors longed for redemption more than Steph Curry, whose missed three-pointer in the game's final moments had sealed the loss. Winning the 2017 NBA Championship was the only item on the agenda for Steph Curry and the Golden State Warriors.

The new season got off to a disappointing start with their first game against the San Antonio Spurs. It was a humiliating defeat, but Steph and the Warriors knew there was no time to hang their heads in shame. If they wanted to win the Championship, they would have to be relentless and hit back hard. They did exactly this by winning their next four games. Luckily, Steph was not the only gifted player for the Warriors. There was, of course, Klay Thompson, with whom Steph had established excellent rapport. The Golden State Warriors also had a new small forward who had been eager to play on their team – none other than Kevin Durant, once a collegiate rival of Steph Curry's. However, the two players were no longer rivals. They were now teammates and their goal was to work together, utilizing and bouncing off each other's strengths to win the Championship.

Such was the comradery amongst Steph, Klay, and Kevin, that they, along with Draymond Green, were to participate in the 2017 NBA All-Star Game. Steph Curry was serious about winning and even his fiercest critics were clenching their teeth. After defeating the Brooklyn Nets in February, the Golden State Warriors were once again in the playoffs. They were on the road to the Championship.

As fate would have it, the rivalry between the Golden State Warriors and the Cleveland Cavaliers was to feature once again as the teams faced each other in the 2017 NBA Championship tournament. This was the third year in a row that they were to face each other. Each team had secured one Championship, and this year would mark the truly dominant team of the NBA. The Cleveland Cavaliers were hell-bent on maintaining their Championship status and securing another title. The Golden State Warriors had only one focus in mind: to redeem themselves by defeating the Cleveland Cavaliers and reclaiming the Championship. In the previous year, the teams played a total of seven games, with the Cleveland Cavaliers securing their victory in that final game. This time, the Golden State Warriors were determined to win their Championship title in less than seven games. They did not want another close call. For the Cleveland Cavaliers, the goal was the same.

The first game of the 2017 NBA Championship occurred on the first of June. The game was played in familiar territory, the Oracle Arena in Oakland, California. While their home arena brought the Warriors comfort, it also brought them the added pressure. They had faced a humiliating defeat the previous year, and now all eyes were on them. In particular, all eyes were on the Warriors' point guard, Steph Curry, who did not live up to his reputation and could not manage to secure another Championship title for his team in 2016. He was under immense pressure to redeem himself.

Luckily, Steph was not alone and he had his teammates on his side. Realizing that his shooting needed practice, Steph decided his focus in the first game would be to aid his teammates with assists, passing them the ball so that they could score baskets.

The game was close. At halftime, the Golden State Warriors were up but by a small margin. The Cleveland Cavaliers were on their tail, and tensions were high. The third quarter belonged solely to the Golden State Warriors, who went on a 13-0 run. Steph had managed to score 28 points in this game, although he seemed to be mostly focused on assists. His assists paid off as he sent the ball many times to Kevin Durant, who managed to score 38 points, the highest amount for Golden State and the highest amount for the game as a whole – managing to surpass even LeBron James. Steph held the record for the most assists for this game and it must have been to his pleasure. His humility and grace would become key characteristics in defining his leadership, and these attributes paid off immensely in the first game of the 2017 NBA Championships. The Golden State Warriors won 113-91.

It seemed as if merely winning the NBA Championship was insufficient for the Golden State Warriors. They wanted to create history and set the bar high. With their win of the first game of the 2017 NBA Championship, they had won 13 games in a row. If they won the second game as well, they would set a record for the longest post-season win streak. If they won this game, it would not only bring them closer to the Championship title, but it would give them something else to brag about – icing on the cake.

This time, Steph managed to help his teammates with assists, but also got back into the groove of shooting. It seemed his streak of poor shooting had finally come to an end. Though Kevin Durant held the record for shooting with 33 points, this was only one point ahead of Steph, who scored 32 points and once again held the record for most assists with 11 in total. LeBron James seemed to be the lone star the Cleveland Cavaliers as he held the record for the most points, rebounds, and assists for the team. However, in spite of his best efforts, he was still no match for the dangerous duo that was Steph Curry and Kevin Durant. Steph Curry even managed to outshine perhaps his greatest adversary, the incomparable point guard, Kyrie Irving. The Golden State Warriors defeated the Cleveland Cavaliers again, 132-113.

Winning 14 games in a row postseason is certainly an achievement to boast about. Yet, remarkably, it was insufficient for the Golden State Warriors. Winning 15 games in a row seemed like a greater achievement to them. However, the third game of the series would bring a new challenge. They were no longer in the comfort zone of Oracle Arena. They were now miles away at the Quicken Loans Arena in Cleveland, Ohio. They were on the Cavaliers' turf and though their fans were there to support them, they had the animosity of the Cavaliers and their fans and the city as a whole to confront. Putting someone to shame in one's own home is the ultimate revenge, but all odds were stacked against the Warriors and they would all have to pull their own weight to continue their winning streak.

While the Warriors were in the lead after the first half, the Cavaliers were fierce, and they were not going to accept defeat so easily. The Cavaliers and LeBron James in particular seemed to want to punish the Warriors for the two previous games. After the third quarter, the Cavaliers were leading with 113 points to the Warriors' 107. There were less than three minutes left in the game. It seemed that the Warriors were going to have to accept defeat after their winning streak, but the Warriors knew that they owed their fans more. There was not a single moment spent lamenting the struggle; the team's only focus was to win. It would seem unlikely if it was not witnessed by thousands in the stadium and millions at home, but the Warriors managed to score 11 points in the short span of time left in the game. Kevin Durant once again was the leader in scoring, followed by Klay Thompson, followed by Steph Curry. The dangerous duo of Steph and Kevin had now become a tremendous trio of Steph, Kevin, and Klay, and with 118 points at the buzzer, they had helped the Golden State Warriors secure their third win of the 2017 NBA Championship. This was their fifteenth post-season win, a record which will be a challenge for other teams to match in the years to come.

Merely two days later on the ninth of June, it was time for the fourth game of the Championship. Once again, the game was held at the Quicken Loans Arena. The Cleveland Cavaliers had been put to shame by the Golden State Warriors in their home and they were eager to fight back with a vengeance. It seemed that the Golden State Warriors were on their way to victory, but the Cleveland Cavaliers were determined to ensure that this would not happen. In the very first quarter, the Cavaliers managed to score 49 points, which set a record for the most points earned in any quarter of a finals game. This must have hit a nerve, as for the first time, the Warriors seemed apprehensive. As if this was not enough, the Cavaliers also punished the Warriors by defeating their previous record for the most three-pointers in the first half of a game by scoring 13 in total. LeBron James was in top form and was one of the dominant forces in the game, even managing to surpass Steph Curry with his number of assists. However, the hero of the Cavaliers was the young point guard whom LeBron had taken under his wing, Kyrie Irving. Steph's rival managed to outshine even Kevin Durant by scoring 40 points in total.

Tensions were high, and the game took a turn for the worse. It had become more than a game; it had become a nasty grudge match. Many fouls were called on this evening in June. Kevin Durant was seen as an enemy of the Cavaliers, and they were determined to break him. The Cavaliers' Dahntay Jones was on the bench and hurled insults at Kevin Durant. Later, Kevin Love fouled Kevin Durant and the latter claimed he was struck on the forehead. LeBron James must have found this amusing as he taunted Kevin Durant over this claim. As if matters could not be worse, Steph Curry was not at his best during this game. He was unable to offer much assistance to his teammates and could not help his team as he had envisioned. Though the game was close, it was evident that the Cavaliers had sought a merciless revenge. They ended the Warriors' winning streak with a final score of 137-116.

The Cleveland Cavaliers had given the Golden State Warriors pause. The Warriors were preparing for celebrations, as they were sure they would win the fourth game and become the 2017 NBA Champions. However, the Cavaliers had snatched victory from the jaws of defeat. Cleveland fans were exhilarated; both LeBron James and Kyrie Irving had led the team to victory. As if to diminish the records set by the Warriors, the Cavaliers seemed to not only want to defeat the Warriors, but also set a few records on the way. Excitement toward the Cavaliers had increased ten-fold; eyes were now on LeBron James and fans and pundits were eager to see if the living legend would defend his team's Championship status. Steph Curry was in a state of worry. Perhaps he had taken the Warriors' winning streak for granted, which is what caused him and his teammates to slip during the fourth game. All was not lost, of course, but the Cavaliers had come back with a vengeance and the Warriors would have to put up a good fight if they wanted to reclaim their Championship status.

Fans and pundits alike all had their predictions for the fifth game of the 2017 NBA Championship. The Cleveland Cavaliers supporters must have felt that the team was back in action and that LeBron James would lead them to victory; the Golden State Warriors supporters were loyal to their team but must have been unsure of what would occur. Though the team was on a long winning streak, they had just faced an embarrassing loss. The players seemed to be out of focus; they were not playing their best and it seemed the enmity of the Cleveland Cavaliers had affected them. Steph Curry must have certainly been anxious. He was back in the spotlight, though now there seemed to be a far greater favorable opinion toward LeBron James. Steph had worked very hard to bring the Warriors this far, and he knew he could not repeat his mistakes from the previous year if he wished to lead them to victory.

The fateful day for both the Golden State Warriors and the Cleveland Cavaliers was the ninth of June. The game was held at the Oracle Arena in Oakland. Though this was the Warriors' home arena and had brought them two wins in the finals so far, there was no guarantee that they would repeat the feat. In Game 3, they had embarrassed the Cavaliers by defeating them in their home arena in front of thousands of their fans. The Cavaliers were intent on winning and they wanted to cause the Warriors the same embarrassment that the Warriors had placed upon them. Tensions were high, and not a single expert could predict what the outcome of this game would be. Steph was as prepared as he could be, and before he knew it, there was the tipoff and it was game time.

It was the Cavaliers' Tristan Thompson who made the first basket of the game. The game was off to a tense start and the first quarter was nerve-wracking. Each time the Golden State Warriors scored, the Cleveland Cavaliers answered back. Any time a team was in the lead, the lead was short-lived as the opposing team would outscore them by a small margin. Steph Curry was as tense as all his teammates, but he was focused on winning. He had devised a strategy – that he would serve as the crux of the team in order to lead them to victory. He had become particularly skilled at passing, and decided he would use this to his advantage to serve as a support for his teammates to score.

The second quarter encompassed perhaps the tensest moment of the game. Kyrie Irving attempted to take possession of the ball from the Warriors' David West but ultimately failed. Fellow Cavalier Tristan Thompson tried to help Kyrie but was unable to. In his rage, Tristan pushed David and animosity was evident in both players. They were in each other's faces expressing their rage and their teammates and coaches had to pull them apart. There was a current of anger running throughout both teams and the tension of the game had increased even more.

While the second quarter ended with the Warriors in the lead, there was no cause for them to become cocky. The Cavaliers would not let them rest on their laurels and were vicious in the third quarter. The giants of the Cavaliers, LeBron and Kyrie, both managed to bring the team to the lead during this quarter. By the time the fourth quarter began, Steph Curry was sweating profusely. His heart and head must have been pounding unforgivably. The Cavaliers were up and if they won this game, they could still win the Championship. The Warriors had to win this game to reclaim their title.

Steph Curry and Kevin Durant owned the fourth quarter as they both managed to score well, with Steph sending assists to Kevin allowing him to score whenever possible. However, with each basket that the Warriors scored, it seemed as if the Cavaliers had several baskets to match. Steph knew that this would be a close game just as the seventh game of the previous NBA Final was. He could not take any chances.

There were less than 50 seconds left on the clock. With all odds against them, Steph was a considerable distance from the basket. He had failed in scoring a three pointer in the seventh game of the previous year. Something in his head must have said, 'let me show them I can do it.' And he did. Steph shot the ball. Though the stadium was packed, and the fans' cheers were deafening, it did not render the swoosh of the net inaudible. Steph Curry made the final basket of the game for the Warriors and brought the Golden State Warriors up to 129 points, way ahead of the Cavaliers' 115. The Cavaliers managed to bring their score up by five points, but it was too late. Nine points ahead, the Golden State Warriors had become the 2017 NBA Champions.

Chapter Summary

• 2015 began a rivalry between the Golden State Warriors and the Cleveland Cavaliers.

• 2016 was a disappointment as the Warriors lost the Championship; Steph felt that he had let his team down and he was determined to redeem himself.

• 2017 was the year where the Golden State Warriors won their second NBA Championship and made history.

Conclusion

Stephen Curry continues to play for the Golden State Warriors. Off the court, his family life with Ayesha continues with their daughters Riley and Ryan. Steph's younger brother Seth is now making his mark on basketball, playing as both a shooting guard and point guard for the Dallas Mavericks. Steph's younger sister Sydel is following in their mother's footsteps as she plays collegiate volleyball for Elon University. His parents remain his biggest supporters. His mother Sonya can always be seen cheering for her elder son in the stands and dancing joyously whenever he scores. If his father is not in the stands, he is commentating on the game.

Dell Curry is now a prominent NBA Commentator. Though Steph Curry has reached heights which his father did not, he continues to consider his father as his hero. In the early days, the diminutive Steph would practice endlessly with Dell. Under Dell's guidance, he would shoot hoops until he mastered his craft.

Originally from the South, Steph Curry would go on to become the pride of Oakland, California. Still in his twenties, he has not only become a prominent basketball player – he has become an icon of the sport. His resume contains many achievements within the sport of basketball – from bringing glory to the Golden State Warriors, to representing the United States in international basketball tournaments. He has become more than a basketball player – he has become a symbol of the American Dream. From his humble beginnings, he has become a living legend. During his presidency, President Barack Obama invited Steph Curry to The White House, as even he was enamored by Steph Curry's athletic ability. President Obama held an initiative to fight against malaria, and had Steph speak about the disease – as Steph began donating nets to catch mosquitos in malaria-infected areas.

He went up against a formidable opponent in LeBron James during the games against the Cleveland Cavaliers and has now become a celebrity on par with LeBron. Nationally and internationally, the name Stephen Curry stands for stellar athletic ability, good sportsmanship, and a decent well-rounded public image. Steph's love for Christ continues, and guides him through all facets of his life. In spite of the ups and downs of an athlete's career, Steph has managed to stay focused and overcome all the odds and cross every hurdle to achieve what he has. He has not forgotten that his family is his priority and with the hectic life that any celebrity must endure, he ensures that he spends time with his wife and daughters; so much so that his wife insists that they are the most normal family ever.

Since becoming a major player, Steph has also become an endorser of Under Armor. He has his own range of sneakers under his name which are part of the Under Armor brand. His shoes have become one of the most popular products in the Under Armor range, and have caused the company's stock prices to increase tremendously. Outside of basketball, he enjoys playing golf and has participated in several celebrity golf tournaments.

What is next for Steph Curry is anyone's guess. What one can say is that his Midas Touch has not faded away; he will continue to rise within the world of basketball. In fact, one might argue that just as Michael Jordan is considered a representation of all a basketball player can be, Steph Curry will one day hold that same title.

Basketball players come and go, but it is safe to say that Steph Curry is here to stay.